WOVEN WORDS PUBLISHERS presents

Tales of Emotions by Neha Malhotra

Neha Malhotra is a content writer by profession and poet by heart. She loves to play with words in her everyday life. She is a contributor writer for various online media publications. Neha is an MBA and started her career in digital marketing. Presently, she is working as a content writer for an IT company in her hometown Chandigarh. Tales of Emotions is her first collection of poetry. To discover more about the world of Neha Malhotra, you can follow her Facebook and Instagram page tales of emotions and can explore her blog nehamalhotra.in. You can get in touch with her at nehamalhotra89@yahoo.com

Tales of Emotions

Neha Malhotra

Woven Words Publishers OPC Pvt. Ltd.

Registered Office:

Vill: Raipur, P.O: Raipur Paschimbar,

Dist: Purba Midnapore, Pin: 721401,

West Bengal, India.

Branch Office(Operations): Hyderabad

www.wovenwordspublishers.com

Email: publish@wovenwordspublishers.com

First published by Woven Words Publishers OPC Pvt. Ltd., 2018

Copyright© Neha Malhotra, 2018

POETRY

IMPRINT: WOVEN WORDS FIRE

ISBN 13: 978-93-86897-35-0

ISBN 10: 9386897350

Price: $ 5/₹ 150

Printed and bound in India.

Time

Time is a crazy bird, flies when no one watches,

Days and night pass, and, ages bloom and fade like flows,

All of us receive the same number of hours in a day,

But, most people move ahead during the time that others waste,

Once time flies, it will never be found again,

All you are left with is regret and pain,

Chase your dreams, and fly so high,

Appreciate this TIME before you die.

Life

Life is a journey; we are not here to stay,
Keep moving forward, and go on your own way,

The journey is long; and the road is rough,

only, faith and love, will be enough,

Don't waste time in anger or regret,
Keep joy in your heart, and your needs will be met.

For some, the journey is fast, and for some, the
journey is slow.
And when the journey finally ends, we will claim a
great reward and find everlasting peace, together
with the lord.

Revenge

And slowly, I learned how people take revenge from you.

They smile at you and shower their unconditional love and care.

In the end,

They leave you alone in the midst of the ocean.

Love is a Guest

Love is an uninvited guest

It enters your life when you

Least expect

And leaves when you want to hold it tight

Guess what?

In the end,

 you have to let it go.

My Promise

When the road is long, and the night is dark,

I promise to be there for you, as a shining star,

When the road is lonely, and, has storms and rain

I will take you towards the hope of seeing the light again.

When you feel that your dreams are going to break,

I promise to be there and together we will make it.

When the world will want to see how much you mean to me,

I promise your love will shine in my eyes which they can see.

When you feel down and want to cry,

I will sing a song for you and make you smile,

When you feel weak and restless,

I promise I will support you with all my emotional strength,

No matter how things will be in future,

I promise, you will still have me,

If this promise is not enough for you,

Then I doubt if I am meant for you!

I don't know if you ever loved me,

But I promise I will love you forever.

Forever

They came, they left

But love remains there

That's the thing about love

It never leaves you

It stays somewhere in the corner of the heart

Forever…. Forever….Forever.

What I deserve

They say I don't deserve to be loved

Little they know...

I am a giver, not a taker.

Love has no age

He saw her for the first time at the florist's,
It was the month of December and days were short.
Hello, this old man said to the lady
The lady turned and asked, are you talking to me?

He smiled and said, may I ask you a question?
She smiled and said yes, but only one.
Every day you come here,
Just to buy a red rose.
She replied with a smile, yes, my husband used to
bring me a red rose.
This rose is so beautiful and lovely you can see.

He is no more, but, his memory stays in my heart.
This is why I come here daily and buy a rose.

Every day they start meeting at the florist's.
Every evening they used to go for a walk, or meet at
the coffee shop.

One day, this man decided to open his heart.
He decided to tell her, how much he loves her,
But he didn't know how to start.

One evening they met, and with all his courage he
said

the day I saw you, I swear I fell in love with you.
Please marry me, and I promise to daily bring
flowers to you,
 She scoffed, and said we are in our 80s,
this is not the age for marriages.

He replied, love has no age, my dear.
love is a beautiful feeling to share,
he tried to convince her in every possible manner,
and after a few days , she said ok. For the rest of our
life we will be together,

The weather was beautiful on their wedding night,
and the bed was full of roses, and the moon was
very high,
they both were deeply in love but a little shy.
In the end, on their wedding bed, they both died.

I asked myself , IS it possible to find True love in
such an old age?
My heart replied, darling , LOVE HAS NO AGE.

Life is Beautiful

Emotions are temporary,

Let them come and go

Life is beautiful to enjoy every bit of it.

I don't visit temple anymore

I don't visit temple anymore

You know why?

Because if I can't make a human happy

How will I make an Idol Happy?

Never give up

The road to success is always rough,

Sometimes, it seems easy and sometimes, tough,

But keep moving forward and never give up.

When you face failure and feel some pressure,

Don't stop trying, because time is a treasure.

When the challenges scare you,

Make some time and pray a little.

When you get tired and feel a little disturbed,

Try hard but, never give up.

When close ones don't support,

And you feel alone,

Be like a tree, which always stands alone.

When you try hard, but don't get results

You want to cry, but your tears dry up,

Work harder, but never give up.

Some, get success soon and some, get it late

It doesn't matter, what's your age.

 Cherish your dreams,

It's never too late.

In search of a soul mate

You can find stories in many people.

But you will find poetry only in one person

And that person is going to be your

Soul mate...

I remember you

Sometimes I write to remember you

Sometimes I write to forget you

And

Sometimes I forget the difference.

It happens for a reason

When things go wrong, and you don't know why.

Tears dry up, but you want to cry,

People will come and go, like a season.

Remember, it happens for a reason.

When feelings fade, and responses stop.

Pray to god, and don't lose hope.

When you are the one, who is trying alone,

Then my dear, it's time to move on.

Don't force, or beg them to stay,

Even if your heart feels aches and pain,

Stick to your decision and walk away.

Walking away seems hard, so, the holding on.

Ask god for strength and move on.

It shall pass too, like a season,

Once it's over, you will find it your best decision,

Remember it happens for a reason.

Memories

I carry you with me, not just in my thoughts

But,

In my laugh,

In the winter morning,

In the summer evening,

In the first sip of coffee,

In the last slice of Pizza,

In my grey hair,

And I guess this is how we both will grow

Old together.

Screenshot

In the Era of Screenshots,

I want to be a handwritten letter

In your wallet…

Wish list

When you feel low, but want to fly,

Tell me your wish and I will take you to the sky.

When, at 2am you crave for cake,

Tell me your wish and I will bake.

When you don't get sleep on a Saturday night,

Tell me your wish, and we will go on long drive.

Some days, when you get mood swings, and you
don't feel good,

Tell me your wish, and we will read together your
favorite book.

Due to heavy work schedule when you feel tired,

To cheer you up, I will get a cup of coffee, and we
can talk for hours if you desire.

When you need a break from your daily routine,

Tell me your wish, and we will go for the sightseeing.

If someday, I am not with you,

Look up at the sky; I am that shining star smiling at you.

Tell me your wish, and I will make it come true.

Goodbye

I don't know what is more painful between these two:

Goodbye to someone you love

or

Goodbye to someone who loves you

They won't come back

When they leave you, you will feel

 Emptiness in the heart

Dust in the eye

Hope in the prayer

But you know what?

They won't come back

I repeat they won't come back

And I am not sure if it is easy

for you or not

But you have to clear the mess

on your own.

Forgiveness

Forgiveness is the art of healing,

It works like turmeric, heals the scars.

If you want to save relations,

Try this crazy method called absolution.

When acerbic tone makes wounds deep,

The eyes may be dry but, the heart weeps.

Relationship becomes cold, and their poises tilt.

All we are left with is regret and guilt,

It is not easy to forget what is said and done,

We need time to recover from the pain,

Because in the end, we all are humans!

People once gone, never come back,

Life doesn't stop for anyone,

Forgive them to make them stay,

Remember, in the end they are your loved ones.

Don't hold grudges and anger in your heart,

Forget everything that happens in the past,

Extend a hand to start a fresh,

Remember, forgiveness is the art of healing.

Confession

It was their 3rd friendship anniversary!

Celebration time for them.

Where she bought a friendship band for him,

He purchased a wedding ring for her.

P.S. Friendship day for the one and proposal day for the other

Breakup

After their breakup, she remembers him

with every sip of black coffee and he reminds her with every piece

of cigarette

P.S. He loves black coffee, and she hates smoking.

My dream

The weather was beautiful and the sun was high,

When I saw him; I felt a little shy,

His eyes were deep like a sea,

He smiled when he saw me.

He shared with me his thoughts and hobbies,

After a pause, he asked for forgiveness,

Because in the beginning, he ignored me.

I accepted his apology, and smiled like an idiot,

He is ambitious and hardworking,

And knows how to treat women,

He is a true gentleman, period.

I want to tell him, how much he inspires me,

I am attracted to him for his spiritual and altruistic qualities.

How much I adore and respect him, I wish he could see!

We stared at each other for a moment,

My heart started beating faster,

He held my hand when he got closer to me,

I could feel butterflies in my stomach.

He touched my face with his palm,

My heart was singing when he kissed my forehead,

I woke up next morning, the mirror was laughing at me,

As if he is saying that it was just a dream, and what if he is not in my destiny.

In my heart, there is still faith and hope,

That One day, we'll be together,

Doesn't matter if today we are on two different boats.

The secret to her heart

It was her 26th birthday, but she was not excited

Until at midnight he bought ice-cream for her.

Only he knows the secret to her heart.

Marriage

After getting married

she became the wife to her husband

Mother to her children

But for her father

She is still a little girl

And for her mother

She is still an apple of her eye.

Life is a game of chess

Life is like a game of chess,

Play it well and you will get success,

Winning or losing, is a part of the game

In the game of life, you'll face the same.

Life has two sides; one is dark, and the other is bright,

Like in a game of chess team one is black and other is white

Side dark implies fear and difficulties

While other side implies optimism and opportunities

Game of chess is like an art

To play it well,

You need both; mind and heart,

Life is like a game of chess,

Changes with each move,

Similarly, in the game of life, sometimes you win and sometimes you lose.

In the end, no matter who left with you;

Bishop or queen,

The moment you checkmate, you have won.

Similarly, in the game of life, no matter who stands with you;

Your friend or even if you are alone,

The moment you defeat your fear; you will achieve your goal.

Never Lose Hope

Never lose hope if you fail

Because

In the end,

The faith survived

 Where the dreams are real

Sorry society - for disappointment!

I'm told that

The deadline for graduation is 18

The deadline to get a job is 20

The deadline to get married is 25

But,

Nobody told me

What is the deadline to fulfil dreams?

The dream to fly

The desire to love and to be loved

The hopes to laugh, cries, learn and grow

Sorry society!

My dreams do not need any deadline

They are free-bird, and I cannot keep them

In a cage;

So, let me live, let me dream, and let me fly high...

Friendship

Friendship is important in any relationship.

It has one simple rule;

Together we laugh, and together we weep.

Friendship is the main ingredient in love's recipe;

It brings you closer to your beloved,

Like aroma coming out of clove.

Friendship is nurtured with trust and patience,

It brings transparency, and love in relations.

Friendship is tested when life gets tough,

Once you pass the test; you get friends for life,

And that is enough.

Friends are support systems of life,

Ups and downs come in life, and friends together survive.

One day we all will get old, and slowly die.

Once we are gone, we will never come back.

Enjoy this time before the final goodbye.

Being strong woman

The journey of woman; is both easy and hard,

She is beautiful, but, also has some scars,

She knows how to use both; her mind and heart.

Being a strong woman is not an easy task,

It takes a lot of courage, and a strong heart.

When life puts her down, and tears her apart,

She stands up again, and fight like a star,

She is both; beautiful and smart.

Being a strong woman is not an easy task,

It takes a lot of courage, and a strong heart.

She gets hurt by the people she loves the most,

But she forgives them because she loves them a lot,

During sunshine, she blooms like a flower,

But at night she puts her face in the pillow and cries hard.

Being a strong woman is not an easy task,

It a takes a lot of courage, and a strong heart.

Often men get physically attracted towards her,

Either a man wants to taste her lips, or wants a one-night stand.

But with courage, she always said no to them without any fear.

She is finding a man worth waking up to, and she is waiting for a godly man

Being a strong woman is not an easy task,

It a takes a lot of courage, and a strong heart.

Never say goodbye

I was standing near the sea, and looking up at the sky,

My heart was filled with pain, and tears were in my eyes,

Cold breeze and rain drops; when touched my face,

I felt like you are saying; I am always with you, darling, so never say goodbye.

I remember, those days and nights we spent together,

All those sorrows and laughter; we have gone through in all weathers,

But, now these lonesome days and nights make me cry,

I remember your words, I am always with you, darling, so never say goodbye.

Every time I visit our photo album, I feel much better,

It reminds me of those vows and promises, we have made together.

47

I found a photo, where you were trying to style my hair,

And in the end, we both burst out with laughing, even today that makes me smile,

While cherishing those memories, a tear rolled down my eye,

It reminds me of your words, I'm always with you, darling, so never say goodbye.

Without you, it is very hard for me to sleep at night,

I wish I could tell you, how much I miss the cuddling and those pillow fights.

Every night that I miss you, I look for you in the sky;

that shining star, reminds me of your words, I'm always with you, darling, so never say goodbye.

I know we will meet again, at some other place beyond the sky,

Where I lie in your arms, and feel your touch, and close my eyes.

Until then, you will stay in my heart; alive, and I will not say goodbye.

Soul mates

She believes in spirituality,

He is the man with altruistic qualities,

Two different people with same traits;

And they never knew,

That they both are soul mates.

She hides him in her poetry, and he hides her in his art.

They both are confessions away, and miles apart.

They are tied together with fate,

And they never knew, that they both are soul mates.

Waiting for him, she spends her days,

He is searching the crowds for her face,

His eyes familiar to her, so her smile familiar to him

But every time, they ignored their intuitions, and walked away.

And they never knew, that they both are soul mates

Today they are not together, but Destiny will reunite them someday.

And then they will walk through life together; all night and day.

And the whole world will know, that they both are soul mates.

I wish I met you first

I wish I had met you, when we were young and innocent,

But we met, when I was aware of the lies, disloyalty, and Heartbreak

I wish I had met you when I trusted people blindly,

But we met when the doubts overshadow Faith,

I wish I could be the first one, with whom you share your passion and fear,

As for now, I want someone to ignore the world, and listen to me with patience and love.

I wish we had met me during your downfall; I would have handled you with emotional strength.

But as for now I would love you, and be happy if you lift me up and become my strength.

I wish I had met you, when a smile was enough to fall in love.

As for now, I don't know the difference between love and lust.

I wish I had met you, when I loved to make someone feel special,

As for now, I need someone to chase me and cherish my love,

I wish you had met me, when I was happy being anyone's last priority,

As for now, I want to be someone's first and only priority.

I am not ready for the halfhearted love, and feelings.

I crave for pure love and a pure soul,

And I wish for more, and more, and more,

I wish you had met me, when I was filled with confidence to conquer a world.

But now, I want you to conquer my heart with your love.

Soldier Never Dies

If I don't come back from the battle field,

Hand over to my mother this letter,

And ask her not to cry,

His son was a soldier, and

Soldiers never die.

If you meet my dad,

Hug him tight on my behalf,

Ask him not to lose strength.

For the one last time,

His son needs his shoulder to ride.

My younger brother is like my own child,

He knows, how much I love his smile,

Hand over my bike keys to him,

And tell him to drive safe and never cry.

My beloved lives in next door,

Hand over these bangles and bridal gown to her,

And apologize on my behalf,

As I couldn't make her my bride.

Tell her my last wish is to see her,

On my last ride.

My last message is for my nation,

I strived hard to serve you, every single time.

Though my role is over in a physical form,

But, you can find me in every soldier;

As a soldier never dies.

The Last Letter

In midst of the ocean,

When I was alone,

Thinking of you, in the cold weather,

I have found you in your last letter,

While the wounds were healed,

But the memories were young,

Smile on the face, but eyes were filled with tears,

I have found you in your last letter.

The emotions and feelings; you never expressed,

I waited long enough for you to say, to flatter me,

At last, I have found them in your last letter.

If we could love each other, instead of being
judgmental,

Maybe we can,

It seems like there is a hope of being together,

I felt this when I found your last letter.

There is a fear I have,

Fear of losing myself in your memories,

I know it is a strange emotion,

But, it is an honest confession,

Don't want to lose your last letter.

Love that was never mine

In the hope of light,

When the sun shines so bright,

I saw him for the first time,

He was the love that was never mine.

I am told that I am fire,

And he is an old wine,

That's the beauty of love,

It never gets old with time.

Though he was the love,

That was never mine,

Never ignore the silence of the first kiss,

Never lose the hope of being together,

It is hard to learn this lesson,

When you have a fear of separation,

I pray to almighty,

To shower him with blessings,

He is happy and alive,

That is enough for me,

So what, if he is a love that was never mine.

Oh! Mother Don't kill me inside

I am a seed in your womb,

Your baby, your daughter,

I want to see the world through your eyes,

Please mother don't kill me inside.

I am a part of you since three months,

I can feel the voice of your anklets and bangles,

I smile when dad says; you are beautiful in your ear,

You can't imagine,

How much I am excited to see you in real.

Don't you want to see me grow?

Don't you want to see me walking in those tiny shoes?

Don't you want me to call you mum for the first time?

If yes, then why do you want me to kill inside?

Why they want us to be apart?

Just because I am a girl?

I am in pain, I am crying,

Give me a chance to live this beautiful Life.

Oh mother!

Don't kill me inside.

But if you still want me to die,

I promise I won't complain,

Because I love you so much, mother,

But I promise I won't let you forget me ever.

He: We all need a friend with whom we can share our ups and down.

She: At the end of the day, you have to be your own best friend.

Being a Rape victim is not a Crime

Those lustful eyes,

Had changed her life,

One horrible night made her alone in a crowd,

Is being a woman a crime?

The scratches on her body made her soul cry,

Almighty is silent,

And society has started judging her character,

And cursing her for being alive.

Shout out to all women,

Being a victim is not an option,

Be a warrior,

And learn how to fight with the demon alone,

Never let the Sita die in you,

But if someone has evil eye on you,

Don't be afraid to awake the Durga in you,

Don't expect from the world to stand for you,

In the end, it is your fight,

Instead of waiting for someone to save you,

Save yourself and be the heroine of your life.

Last sip of Coffee

When I look outside the window,

Birds are dancing as if they have seen you smile,

Flowers are blooming, as if they fall in love with you,

Meanwhile, I am having a last sip of coffee,

While thinking about you.

The memories we had made together,

The thoughts we had shared together,

They are less sweet and strong,

They are like my last sip of coffee.

You are my first morning kiss,

And a late night goodbye,

No matter how far you are from me,

In my dreams you are always near me.

This is the best thing about being in love,

You can feel its presence in its absence too,

That is because our love is stronger,

Like every sip of coffee, I take.

Come let's have a cup of coffee tonight,

In the crumbled bed-sheet,

Let's have a pillow fight,

And enjoy this last sip of coffee together.

I want to grow old with you

When the night is dark, and

We are miles apart,

I will be here waiting for you,

Take me to your heart,

I want to grow old with you.

Hiding, from the rain and snow,

I want to lie down in your arms,

Kiss me hard before I get old,

Take me to your heart,

I want to grow old with you.

Yes, I love you for your strength,

But I love you more, for your scars,
Show me your scars tonight,
let me kiss them for the rest of the life,

I want to grow old with you in every life.

The Feelings May Never Go away

When I was a kid,

They said that pain makes you grow,

But when I have grown old,

Life taught me that pain fades away,

But The Feelings may never go.

The day I had my first kiss,

I felt the Goosebumps,

What if, today my body feels the emptiness,

And my lips have dried up,

The taste of your lips may never go.

When I was young,

All my dreams come true, they wished for me,

They have no idea; you are the only dream,

I wished for.

Keep yourself occupied, they say, to forget your memories,

Little do they know, your memories are on my fingertips,

You are gone,

But your memories may never go.

Walk in My Shoes

Walk a mile in my shoes, and

tell me how you feel.

The rain, the storm, the pain, the struggle,

I have gone through it all, tell me how to heal.

If you want to judge me,

For the decisions I have taken,

Or for the things I have done wrong,

Take a walk in my shoes.

Walk a mile in my shoes, and

Deal with the lies and betrayal;

I have dealt with,

Promise me you won't stumble or get scared.

The things I have gone through,

The pain almighty had put me through,

If you think it is not a big deal for you,

Then I would like to ask you,

Take a walk in my shoes.

Can Love Happen Twice?

A little girl who loves to sleep,

Wakes up every night to ask herself,

Can love happen twice?

In the war of love,

She had lost her dignity and self-respect,

She waited long enough to earn them back,

But it seems like the demon won the game.

One beautiful evening,

She met a guy with a beautiful smile,

He made her question in the first meeting;

Can love happen twice?

Never stop searching for love,

Soul mates do exist in this beautiful world,

What if you failed in first attempt?

Take it as a lesson for life.

Keep looking for love, because you never know,

The right one might be waiting for you in another corner,

He will come into your life like a beautiful poem,

And will make you believe, that yes, love can happen twice.

You are My Morning Thought

Let me take you to the world of thoughts,

Where the silence speaks, and eyes listen,

Where the heart beats on the rhythm of emotions,

Let me take you to the dream of thoughts,

That will make you sleep with a smile

On your lips;

And will wake you up in the morning,

With the first sip of coffee.

Whether it is a summer morning

Or winter evening,

The thoughts will often visit and

Stay in my mind;

The thought of being with you forever.

When silence kisses darkness,

I can feel your presence;

No it is not just a thought,

It is a connection of a lifetime that bound us together,

Forever and ever.

I wish you stayed little longer

Rainbow is smiling through my window,

Waving you goodbye,

I wish you stayed a little longer; like this lonely night,

I have mischievous stories to tell,

I want to love you a little more than yesterday,

I wish you stayed little longer; like this lonely night,

I wish I could hug you, for one last time,

I wish I could taste your lips tonight,

I wish you stayed a little longer; like this lonely night,

I love the way we fight for the last slice of pizza,

I love when you kiss my forehead every day,

I want to cherish those moments with you,

I wish you stayed a little longer; like this lonely
night,

Come back, this lonely night is about to be over,

Let's cherish first ray of sun together,

And love each other a little more this time.

With a new day, let's fulfil those promises,

That are left behind;

Please come and stay a little longer this time,

And never leave me alone; like a lonely night.

Love Never Dies

I am tired of this lonesome night,

It seems my love is dying,

I asked moon, have you ever felt the same?

love never dies, he replied.

Every morning sun hides you and shines so bright.

I asked moon, don't you feel betrayed?

Love is forgiving and gentle, no place for complaints.

He smiled and replied,

When love leaves you heartbroken,

And promises fade away,

It seems love is about to die;

I asked moon, Am I right?

Love is freedom and not a possession,

Cherish it without owning it,

This way you will never lose it, he replied.

Life with many carriages

Life is like a train; with many carriages,

We meet strangers but never communicate with them,

Never hesitate in shaking hands,

It is always good to make new friends.

In this journey, some will leave you at one or the other station,

So, nurture your relations with love and patience.

Once people go, they never come back.

So, tell them now that how much you love or admire them.

I don't know if we meet again in this journey or not,

But I will always pray to almighty,

To bless you with strength and happiness.

Let it go

This coming and going of people,

Breaks heart in million pieces,

To get rid of this pain,

The heart decides to let it go.

Do the clouds ever fall in love with sea?

Did you ever love me?

I'm told not,

And it kills me a little bit inside.

The sunset is over, and so are our dreams

Of being together;

No hope and desire are left anymore,

Finally, the heart decided to let it go.

Can I hold your hand for one last time?

Can I tell the whole world that you are mine?

I'm told that it is not possible in this lifetime,

Never mind, I will wait for you in the next lifetime,

But I can't live with the pain of separation anymore,

If you ask me, I am still waiting for you,

They say I should move on now,

So, my heart decided to let it go.

Forget me if you can

You want to forget me,

I understand;

If a flower can forget its fragrance,

Moon can forget its shine,

You can forget me if you can.

If you try to forget me with every night,

Make sure I am not staying in your mind,

Like a seed planted in soil can do wonders,

I am prepared to expect wonders,

From the love you are hiding from me.

If you want to remember me as a memory,

Well, you have already become a memory for me,

But my essence will never fade till eternity,

No matter if I become a star in the sky,

Still if you want to forget me you can try.

I am told I am an ocean of love,

And you are standing near the shore,

Waiting to kiss me,

I will climb up your lips,

And feed you with love,

To make our love stronger with every bite.

This is how I will become a part of your soul,

And will flow within you like blood in your veins,

I will keep you in my arms for infinity,

And never let you forget me,

But if you want to forget me, you can try.

A Cup of Conversation

She: How to deal with the struggle of life?

He: You don't need to deal with it. You need to learn from it.

She: Why do people think that only a broken heart can be a poet?

He: Because they do not know the difference between a broken heart and creative heart.

He: Do you believe in fairytales?

She: Yes, but with a twist.

He: twist?

She: he will come in Military uniform instead of ethnic wear.

Society: 28 and still single?

She: 28 and can buy my own diamonds.

He: Being loved or being cherished?

She: Being cherished any day!

He: Do you believe in love at first sight

She: Yes, every time when I see pizza with extra cheese.

She: What never go out of style?

He: Simplicity!

He: Let's go to a movie.

She: Let's go for a long walk and get lost in the city.

She: who is the biggest enemy of a woman?

He: society?

She: Another woman.

She: What makes you grounded?

He: Knowing the truth, that people will leave you if you keep your nose up in the air.

He: Sometimes life sucks!

She: Take a nap! You will be alright.

He: Why do you always talk about sleep?

She: Because sleeping is the best medicine, I believe.

He: Why do lovers always talk about the moon and the stars?

She: Maybe because they haven't tasted pizza and muffins yet!

He: Hahaha. Okay, then let me take you to have some pizza and muffins.

He: How to handle yourself when life knocks you down?

She: Get up! Wipe your tears and tell yourself that life has better plans for you.

She: What is your guilt?

He: Things I left Unsaid.

He: You know what the worst thing that can happen to a man is?

She: What?

He: Living life on someone else terms and conditions.

He: The world is crazy.

She: Why?

He: They want to be a part of your success but want to be a part of your failure.

She: Do you believe in a distance relationship?

He: Yes!

She: Example?

He: A soldier and his beloved.

He: Why are you like this?

She: Like what?

He: Outspoken

She: I am sarcastic too!

She: What is the best thing about your relationship?

He: We try to win each other even after so many years of our marriage.

She: What is more dangerous- being nice or being honest?

He: Fake Promise!

He: He praises the beauty of every woman he meets, but he never compliments you. Don't you get jealous?

She: The way he looks at me, his eyes says it all (*Blushed*).

He: If I get a chance, I want to be her Monday Morning.

She: Why not on Saturday evening?

He: There are ample people around her, who wanted to be her Saturday evening. But I am sure, she is waiting for someone who can be her Monday morning.

He: Tit for tat is fair in love and war.

She: Honey, revenge can never heal a broken heart.

He: you are a Jhandu Baam

She: why? Because I take a long time to understand things?

He: No, because you are a healer.

Author's Note

This book has been a very long and emotional journey on which I have tried to take my readers along with me. My main inspiration for this book was how we sometimes stand as witnesses to all the havoc these emotions can create in somebody's life. It has always fascinated me how every person reacts differently to the same situations and different kind of emotions it provokes in them. Writing this book was a dream of mine which could not have been possible without the support of all my family and friends. Thank you for all the endless support and encouragement and having faith in me when I needed it the most. Especially, to three pillars of my life – My brother and my cousins – Mohit Malhotra, Amit Malhotra, and Ankit Malhotra for always believing in my dreams and motivating me. Last but not the least I want to thank all my amazing readers who chose to read this book. I always believe authors always bare a piece of them in their work which creates this beautiful connection with their readers.

Thanks for all the love and you can keep in touch with me and my other work through all my social links mentioned.

Love
Neha Malhotra

For more, visit www.wovenwordspublishers.com

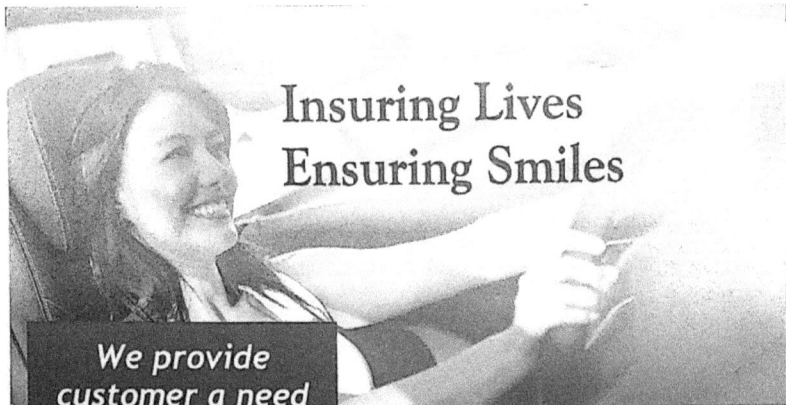

Insuring Lives
Ensuring Smiles

We provide customer a need base solutions to all their insurance and investment needs for better returns and future requirements like children education and marriage, retirement, by advicing them for good return investments.

insurednow

Mohit Malhotra
Res: HE 139A, First Floor, Phase 7, Mohali.
Mob: 7888348542, 9872481839

OUR PRODUCTS

1. Family Protection
2. Children Education
3. Children Marriage
4. Retirement
5. Health Insurance
6. Accidental Insurance
7. Critical care
8. Vehicle Insurance
9. Travel Insurance
10. Household & Building Insurance
11. Business and Shop Insurance

www.ingramcontent.com/pod-product-compliance
Lightning Source LLC
Chambersburg PA
CBHW032112040426
42337CB00040B/259